DINOSAURS

DILOPHOSAURUS

BY CHELSEA XIE

Kids Core

An Imprint of Abdo Publishing
abdobooks.com

abdobooks.com

Published by Abdo Publishing, a division of ABDO, PO Box 398166, Minneapolis, Minnesota 55439.

Printed in the United States of America, North Mankato, Minnesota.
102023
012024

THIS BOOK CONTAINS RECYCLED MATERIALS

Cover Photo: Daniel Eskridge/Shutterstock Images
Interior Photos: Jose Antonio Penas/Science Source, 4–5; James Kuether/Science Source, 6; Detlev van Ravenswaay/Science Source, 9; Karl Aage Isaksen/Shutterstock Images, 10; Daniel Eskridge/Shutterstock Images, 12–13; Carver Mostardi/Alamy, 15; Shutterstock Images, 17, 28–29; Mircea Moira/Shutterstock Images, 18; Pat Canova/Alamy, 20–21; Red Line Editorial, 22; Nikreates/Alamy, 25; Christian Puntorno/Shutterstock Images, 26

Editor: Marley Richmond
Series Designer: Mary Shaw

Library of Congress Control Number: 2023939658

Publisher's Cataloging-in-Publication Data

Names: Xie, Chelsea, author.
Title: Dilophosaurus / by Chelsea Xie
Description: Minneapolis, Minnesota: Abdo Publishing, 2024 | Series: Dinosaurs | Includes online resources and index.
Identifiers: ISBN 9781098292676 (lib. bdg.) | ISBN 9798384910619 (ebook)
Subjects: LCSH: Dinosaurs--Juvenile literature. | Prehistoric animals--Juvenile literature. | Dilophosaurus--Juvenile literature.
Classification: DDC 567.90--dc23

CONTENTS

Small groups of *Dilophosaurus* lived together.

CHAPTER 1

A FIERCE HUNTER

A *Dilophosaurus* (deye-LOH-fuh-SOHR-uhs) runs through the forest on two legs. Claws on its feet sink into the soft ground. The creature lets out a loud roar. It towers over the bushes. The two crests on the top of its head brush against leaves in the trees.

Dilophosaurus had longer arms than other two-legged dinosaurs. This feature probably helped it catch fish.

The *Dilophosaurus* reaches a deep river. The splash of a large fish catches its attention. The *Dilophosaurus* plunges its arms into the water. It strikes the fish with sharp claws.

The fish tries to escape, but it can't. The *Dilophosaurus* is too powerful. It grips the fish in its strong hands. It lowers its head, ready to enjoy a fresh meal. The *Dilophosaurus* tears into the meat with its sharp teeth.

About Dinosaurs

Dilophosaurus was a dinosaur. Dinosaurs first lived about 252 million years ago. The period when dinosaurs were alive is called the Mesozoic era. This era can be split into the Triassic, Jurassic, and Cretaceous periods.

Dinosaurs went **extinct** at the end of the Cretaceous period. The Cretaceous period was 145 million to 66 million years ago. *Dilophosaurus* lived about 201 million to 175 million years ago. That was the early part of the Jurassic period.

All dinosaurs were reptiles. Examples of reptiles today include crocodiles, lizards,

What Caused Dinosaurs' Extinction?

Scientists are not sure why dinosaurs went extinct. Many believe that a large space rock called an asteroid crashed into Earth. The impact caused dust to fill the sky. It blocked the Sun and changed the climate. This made it difficult for living things to survive, including dinosaurs.

About 66 million years ago, an asteroid struck Earth near the coast of modern-day Mexico. It may have caused dinosaurs to go extinct.

and snakes. Once, there were many types of dinosaurs. Some walked on four legs. Others stood on two feet. Some dinosaurs ate only plants. Other dinosaurs were fierce **predators**.

Some parks and museums create life-size models of dinosaurs, such as *Dilophosaurus*.

Birds are the only surviving **descendants** of dinosaurs.

Dilophosaurus roamed on two legs. It mainly ate other animals, including fish. *Dilophosaurus* **fossils** have been found in the present-day United States. Scientists use fossils to learn more about these creatures.

PRIMARY SOURCE

Adam Marsh is a scientist. He has studied *Dilophosaurus* fossils. This is how he described the dinosaur:

> *Dilophosaurus* is clearly built for being a big [predator]. It's a large-bodied animal that was built for eating other animals.

Source: John Pickrell. "'Jurassic Park' Got Almost Everything Wrong about This Iconic Dinosaur." *National Geographic*, 7 July 2020, nationalgeographic.com. Accessed 9 Mar. 2023.

Comparing Texts

Think about the quote. Does it support the information in this chapter? Or does it give a different perspective? Explain how in a few sentences.

Fossils do not show what color a dinosaur was. Scientists aren't sure what color the crests of *Dilophosaurus* were.

CHAPTER 2

DILOPHOSAURUS APPEARANCE

It is difficult to know exactly what *Dilophosaurus* looked like. People were not alive when dinosaurs lived. Scientists learn about the appearance of *Dilophosaurus* from fossils.

Fossils are rare. Skin, fur, and feathers break down easily.

Hard body parts, such as bones, are more likely to become fossils. Scientists have found only *Dilophosaurus* bones and teeth. They do not know if the dinosaur had scales or feathers.

This dinosaur had two crests on its head. The name *Dilophosaurus* means "two-crested lizard." The crests were likely covered in keratin. This is the same material that is found in human hair and fingernails.

Dinosaur Feathers

Scientists once thought that dinosaurs looked like giant lizards. They believed that dinosaurs were covered only in scales. But in the 1990s, scientists found dinosaur fossils that seemed to show feathers. Now, scientists believe that many kinds of dinosaurs had feathers.

Dinosaur tracks can also be fossilized. *Dilophosaurus* tracks have been found in Arizona.

Scientists have several ideas about *Dilophosaurus* head crests. The crests may have been used for display. Scientists think they were brightly colored and helped to attract mates.

Bones and Teeth

Scientists study *Dilophosaurus* skeletons. They know these dinosaurs were big. *Dilophosaurus* was one of the largest dinosaurs of the early Jurassic period. It was about 25 feet (7.6 m) long and 8 feet (2.4 m) tall. The dinosaur weighed about 660 pounds (300 kg).

Despite its large size, scientists believe *Dilophosaurus* moved quickly. The dinosaur's skeleton had similarities to a bird's skeleton. Birds have air sacs that connect to their lungs. These provide birds with oxygen so they can move quickly. There is evidence that *Dilophosaurus* had air sacs too. The bones near their lungs had indents where air sacs would have fit. But air sacs are made of soft **tissue**.

The Geological Museum in Warsaw, Poland, has a model of *Dilophosaurus*.

Dilophosaurus had long, thin teeth. Some scientists think this meant it would not have eaten large animals.

They do not fossilize easily. Scientists must use other fossils to make guesses about the dinosaur's body and behavior.

Fossils of sharp teeth show that *Dilophosaurus* ate meat. The dinosaur's jaw is shaped like a crocodile's jaw. *Dilophosaurus* had a strong bite. Scientists cannot know for certain what animals *Dilophosaurus* ate. But the dinosaurs likely ate fish.

Explore Online

Visit the website below. Does it give any new information about *Dilophosaurus* that wasn't in Chapter Two?

Dilophosaurus

abdocorelibrary.com/dilophosaurus

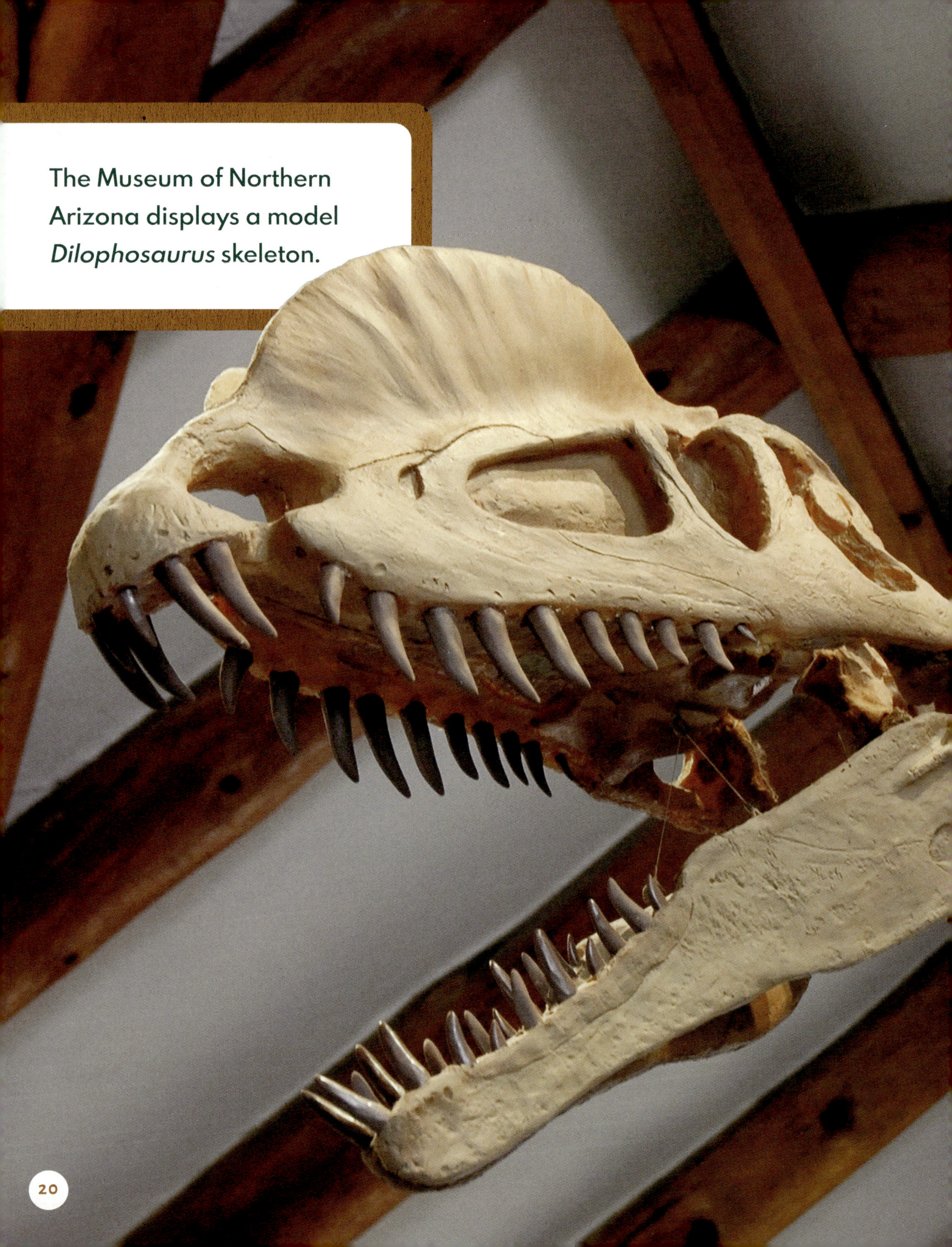

The Museum of Northern Arizona displays a model *Dilophosaurus* skeleton.

CHAPTER 3

FOSSIL RECORDS

A man named Jesse Williams discovered the first *Dilophosaurus* fossils in 1940. Williams was a member of the Navajo Nation. He found the fossilized bones on Navajo land in northern Arizona.

Where *Dilophosaurus* Lived

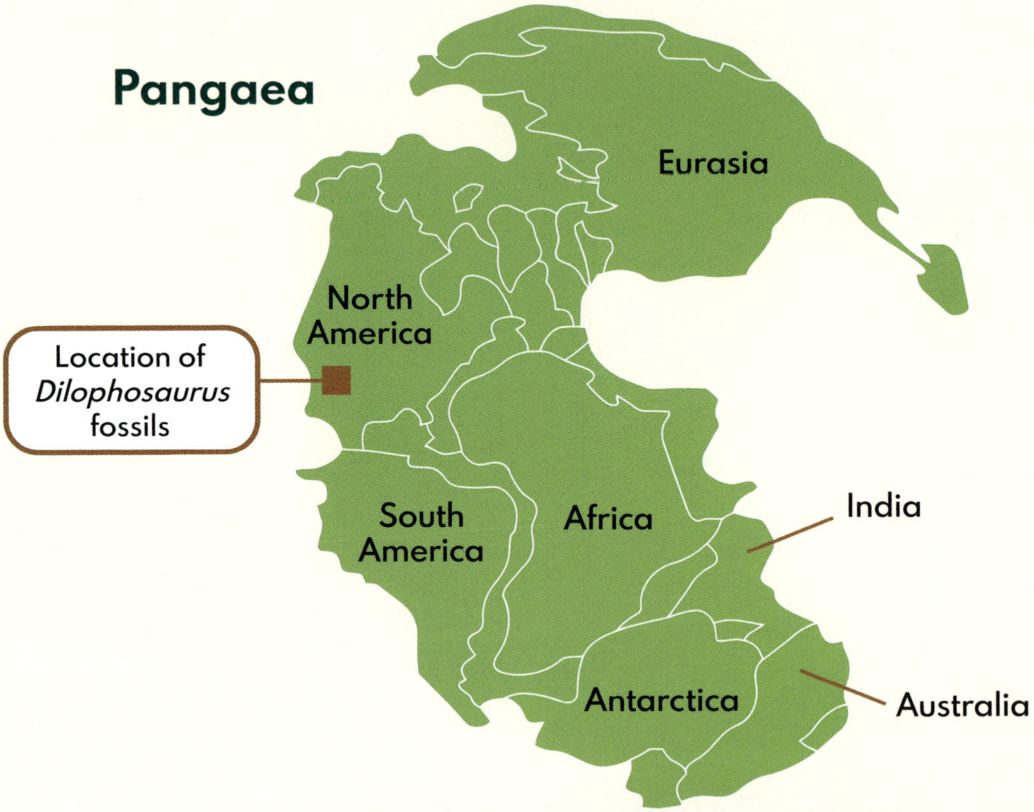

A long time ago, all the land on Earth was connected in a supercontinent called Pangaea. *Dilophosaurus* lived in a small region of Pangaea. Their fossils have been found in present-day Arizona.

Williams showed a paleontologist named Sam Welles the remains. A paleontologist is a scientist who studies fossils. Welles and his team removed the fossils from the ground. They uncovered bones that made up the dinosaur's legs, arms, and spine. They also found pieces of the dinosaur's skull.

At first, Welles thought the fossils belonged to the dinosaur *Megalosaurus*. Then, Welles found more fossils in Arizona. He found fossils of the dinosaur's crests. He realized the fossils he had been studying were not *Megalosaurus*.

Ready for Display

It takes many steps to prepare fossils for display. First, the large pieces of rock that contain the fossils are dug up. The rocks are covered in hard plaster for protection. They are moved to labs. There, scientists use special tools to chip away at the rock until they reveal the fossil.

It was an undiscovered type of dinosaur. Welles named it *Dilophosaurus* in 1970.

Today, *Dilophosaurus* skeletons are on display at the University of California Museum of Paleontology. This is where Welles worked. The fossils belong to the Navajo Nation.

Dilophosaurus in Media

Dilophosaurus is well-known for its role in the 1993 film *Jurassic Park*. This movie was based on a book by Michael Crichton. However, both the book and film versions of *Dilophosaurus* are much different from the actual creature. One noticeable difference is the size. In the film, *Dilophosaurus* is about the size of a dog. This is much smaller than *Dilophosaurus* really was.

Some parks have *Dilophosaurus* models that include neck frills. But scientists have found no evidence that the dinosaur had this feature.

Another key difference is that the *Dilophosaurus* in the movie has a neck frill. Fossils do not show that *Dilophosaurus* had this body part. Steven Spielberg was the director of *Jurassic Park*. He added this feature to the creature. He was inspired by a type of lizard in Australia that has a frill. In the movie, *Dilophosaurus* can spit **venom**. This behavior was also described in Crichton's book. He took the idea for this ability from cobras.

Reptiles such as turtles often move slowly. But scientists think most dinosaurs would have moved more quickly, similar to birds.

Jurassic Park correctly showed some facts. The film showed the dinosaur's crests. In *Jurassic Park, Dilophosaurus* is quick. Many people had thought dinosaurs behaved like modern-day reptiles. They pictured them as slow and lazy. Some people still think this. But paleontologists know that dinosaurs moved more like birds. *Jurassic Park* was the first time a major film showed dinosaurs moving this way.

Scientists have found fossils from about 700 types of dinosaurs. Fossils show what dinosaurs may have looked like. Scientists look at *Dilophosaurus* fossils to learn more about these creatures. The fossils give scientists clues about how the animal may have behaved. Understanding dinosaurs helps scientists understand how the world was a long time ago. These ancient creatures continue to interest all kinds of people.

Further Evidence

Look at the website below. Does it give any new evidence to support Chapter Three?

What Is a Paleontologist?

abdocorelibrary.com/dilophosaurus

DINO DETAILS

Brightly colored crests used to attract mates
Powerful jaws and sharp teeth to tear into meat
Strong arms to firmly grip the animals it ate

Index

About the Author

Chelsea Xie is a writer who lives in San Diego, California. She enjoys reading poetry and spending time outdoors.

Brightly colored crests used to attract mates
Powerful jaws and sharp teeth to tear into meat
Strong arms to firmly grip the animals it ate

Glossary

descendants
creatures that share the same ancestor

extinct
no longer exists

fossil
the remains of very old animals or plants

predator
an animal that hunts other animals

tissue
a group of cells in an animal or plant body that are like each other and do similar things

venom
a poisonous substance

Online Resources

To learn more about *Dilophosaurus*, visit our free resource websites below.

Core Library CONNECTION
FREE! COMMON CORE MULTIMEDIA RESOURCES

Visit **abdocorelibrary.com** or scan this QR code for free Common Core resources for teachers and students, including vetted activities, multimedia, and booklinks, for deeper subject comprehension.

Booklinks NONFICTION NETWORK
FREE! ONLINE NONFICTION RESOURCES

Visit **abdobooklinks.com** or scan this QR code for free additional online weblinks for further learning. These links are routinely monitored and updated to provide the most current information available.

Learn More

Extraordinary Dinosaurs and Other Prehistoric Life. DK, 2022.

Hulick, Kathryn. *Dinosaurs.* Abdo, 2023.

Index

About the Author

Chelsea Xie is a writer who lives in San Diego, California. She enjoys reading poetry and spending time outdoors.